TEENS IN SAUDI ARABIA

Teens in Saudi Arabia

by Nicki Yackley-Franken

Content Adviser: Christopher Rose, M.A.,
Outreach Coordinator,
Center for Middle Eastern Studies,
University of Texas at Austin

Reading Adviser: Katie Van Sluys, Ph.D.,
Department of Teacher Education,
DePaul University

Compass Point Books ✵ Minneapolis, Minnesota

Compass Point Books
3109 West 50th Street, #115
Minneapolis, MN 55410

Editor: Julie Gassman
Designers: The Design Lab and Jaime Martens
Photo Researcher: The Design Lab
Geographic Researcher: Lisa Thornquist, Ph.D.
Cartographer: XNR Productions, Inc.
Library Consultant: Kathleen Baxter

Art Director: Jaime Martens
Creative Director: Keith Griffin
Editorial Director: Carol Jones
Managing Editor: Catherine Neitge

Library of Congress Cataloging-in-Publication Data
Yackley-Franken, Nicki.
Teens in Saudi Arabia / by Nicki Yackley-Franken.
p. cm. — (Global connections)
Includes bibliographical references and index.
ISBN-13: 978-0-7565-2066-3 (library binding)
ISBN-10: 0-7565-2066-5 (library binding)
ISBN-13: 978-0-7565-2074-8 (paperback)
ISBN-10: 0-7565-2074-6 (paperback)
   1. Teenagers—Saudi Arabia—Social conditions—Juvenile literature.
   2. Teenagers—Saudi Arabia—Social life and customs—Juvenile
   literature. 3. Saudi Arabia—Social conditions—21st century—Juvenile
   literature. 4. Saudi Arabia—Social life and customs—21st century—
   Juvenile literature.   I. Title.
   HQ799.S32Y33 2007
   305.23509538—dc22   2006027062

Visit Compass Point Books on the Internet at www.compasspointbooks.com
or e-mail your request to custserv@compasspointbooks.com.

Table of Contents

Mediterranean Sea

Black Sea

GREECE

Caspian Sea

KAZAKHSTAN

L. Balkhash

TURKEY

GEORGIA

ARMENIA

AZERBAIJAN

UZBEKISTAN

KYRGYZSTAN

LIBYA

CYPRUS

LEBANON

SYRIA

IRAQ

TURKMENISTAN

TAJIKISTAN

ISRAEL

JORDAN

Euphrates

IRAN

EGYPT

ER

L. Chad

CHAD

Red Sea

Nile

KUWAIT

SAUDI ARABIA

BAHRAIN

QATAR

AFGHANISTAN

PAKISTAN

Indus

Ganges

OMAN

SUDAN

C.A.R.

U.A.E.

Congo

ERITREA

OMAN

Arabian Sea

IN

YEMEN

DJIBOUTI

CONGO

ETHIOPIA

SOMALIA

ANGOLA

RWANDA

BURUNDI

UGANDA

L. Victoria

KENYA

SRI

TANZANIA

L. Malawi

INDIAN

OCEAN

MONGOLIA

NORTH KOREA

SOUTH KOREA

Huang

Yellow Sea

East China Sea

CHINA

Yangtze

NEPAL

BHUTAN

BANGLADESH

Salween

MYANMAR

LAOS VIETNAM

Mekong

THAILAND

KAMPUCHEA

Bay of Bengal

PHILIPPINES

South China Sea

BRUNEI

Riyadh ★

LIFE FOR TEENS IN SAUDI ARABIA IS A MIXTURE OF THE PAST AND PRESENT. They live in a country with modern shopping malls and ancient mosques, goat-herding desert dwellers and Mercedes-driving city folks. Officially known as the Kingdom of Saudi Arabia, the nation upholds ancient rituals and cultural ideals, while at the same time it has developed into a modern and industrial country.

Today's teenagers make up the largest portion of the kingdom's total population—an estimated 60 percent of the country's 27 million people are under the age of 20. They are vital to the future of the desert country. Saudi Arabia's continuation as a progressive nation with a strong foundation in religious traditions is very much in the hands of its teens.

The traditional school dress for males is a white, long shirtlike garment.

1

CHAPTER ONE

Lecturing & Listening

AN ALL-FEMALE GROUP OF 17-YEAR-OLD STUDENTS sits in small wooden desks with their pens in constant motion as they take notes. The classroom walls are decorated with colorful science charts and framed pictures containing inspirational messages taken from the Qur'an, Islam's sacred text. A large black chalkboard full of white Arabic writing is positioned in the front of the classroom. The teacher of these second-year high school students explains how Saudi Arabia's founder, Abdul Aziz al Saud, led an army to attack and capture Riyadh in 1902 to create a united Saudi state. The students concentrate on attaining and remembering the facts and figures the teacher recites.

The Islamic Tradition

Saudi Arabians consider their country to be the birthplace of Islam. Muhammad, the founder of Islam, was born in 570 in Mecca, a city located in western Saudi Arabia. According to Islamic tradition, when Muhammad was around 40 years old, the angel Gabriel came to him, telling him that he had been chosen as Allah's (God's) prophet. Allah continued to speak or send messages to Muhammad throughout his life, and Muhammad began to share Allah's words with others. Thus Islam was born. The messages Muhammad received from Allah were later written down, and his teachings now make up the Qur'an, the sacred text.

Dedicated to Education

Saudi Arabians are dedicated to providing their students with a quality education, so leaders constantly work to reform the educational system. Fifty years ago, girls wouldn't even have received an education—the first girls' school did not open in the kingdom until 1963. Saudi education has come a long way since then, and the nation is committed to improving the learning opportunities and environments for all young people.

Since 2002, Saudi Arabian leaders have worked to offer a more comprehensive and effective education. For instance, the government has taken steps to provide a more equal education to female students and to slowly lessen the emphasis placed on religious studies in all levels of schooling. The country has opened a number of schools that offer night classes for teens who have to work during the daytime. Also offered are vocational secondary schools for teenagers who want to learn a trade instead of attending regular high school.

In 2005, the government announced it would spend 276.1 billion *riyals* (U.S.$76 billion) on improving the education system's curriculum, teaching staff, and school facilities. Currently, the government spends nearly 10 percent of its annual gross domestic product on education

riyal
ree-AHL

Though the educational system is reducing the emphasis on religion, special Qur'anic schools continue to focus on Islam and memorization of the Qur'an.

Teen Scenes

A 15-year-old boy walks with his friends on their way to soccer practice after school. The boys walk across the freshly cut lawn of their prestigious all-male high school on their way to the school's full-sized soccer field. The young man just finished computer class. It was his last class of the day and one that will be helpful when he begins working at his father's shipping business in Jeddah.

In a small village nearby, a teen girl waits for her older brother to pick her up from school. Sitting with her notebook open on her lap, she tries to memorize a page of history notes. As the oldest of a date farmer's seven daughters, her father will want her to marry soon after high school to ease financial strain. So she must study hard to prove to her family that she deserves to go to college before marrying and starting a family.

Though boys and girls attend separate schools and face different futures, their educations are similar in structure and quality. The kingdom continues to refine and improve the educational system for both genders.

each year, more than any other Middle Eastern country. For this reason, Saudi teenagers can expect to continue to see improvements in education.

Today the kingdom has around 24,000 public schools and 850 private schools. Students attend six years of primary school from ages 6 to 12, three years of intermediate school from ages 12 to 15, and three years of secondary school from ages 15 to 18.

The majority of school-attending teens go to government-funded public schools, although in recent years, private education has become popular. Like public schools, private schools are monitored by the government, but generally they offer a few extra subjects. Private school students, for instance, often have the opportunity to learn languages other than Arabic or English, such as French, Spanish, or Italian.

In the Classroom

The average school day begins between 6:30 and 7:30 A.M. and continues until between 1:30 and 2:30 P.M. Students attend classes Saturday through Wednesday, and they get a weekend break on Thursday and Friday, the Islamic Sabbath day.

Like almost all elements of Saudi life, schools are segregated according to gender. Boys attend all-male schools, where the teachers and staff members are also male. Girls attend all-female schools, where the majority of teachers are female.

A Country Reads

Money began streaming into Saudi Arabia in the 1970s during the Saudi oil boom. The government decided it needed to dedicate part of its newfound wealth to improving education. In 1960, only 22 percent of boys and 2 percent of girls attended grade schools, and in 1970, only 15 percent of men and 2 percent of women were considered literate, or able to read. To combat this problem, the government devised a plan to spread education to everyone in the kingdom by building thousands of new schools, improving teacher training, and starting adult literacy programs. Because of these efforts, the literacy rate had risen to around 78 percent of the total population and even higher among the youth by 2002. Few governments worldwide have done so much to abolish illiteracy in such a short time.

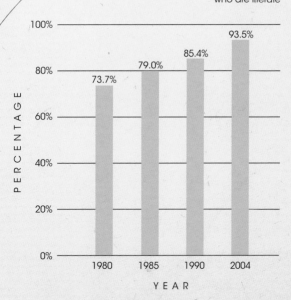

The Growth of Youth Literacy
Percentage of people ages 15 to 24 who are literate

- 1980: 73.7%
- 1985: 79.0%
- 1990: 85.4%
- 2004: 93.5%

PERCENTAGE

YEAR

Source: UN Common Database

Black Gold

Before the 1950s, most Saudis made their living as farmers or animal herders. They did not have proper medical care or access to education. In most respects, the people of Saudi Arabia lived isolated lives. They spent their days trying to survive the country's harsh climate and often dangerous terrain.

But the discovery of oil in the 1930s and the start of large-scale production in the 1940s transformed the country to one of the wealthiest nations in the world. Today, Saudi Arabia is the largest petroleum producer and exporter in the world and possesses 25 percent of all known oil reserves worldwide. Saudi Arabia earned an estimated 557 billion riyals (U.S. $148.5 billion) in revenues from petroleum exports in 2005. Experts anticipate that revenues will continue to climb in the years to come.

During the last few decades, the money from Saudi Arabia's immense oil supplies has resulted in rapid modernization. Government officials began an aggressive plan to turn the kingdom into a developed, industrialized nation. Free public education spread throughout the land and modern medical facilities sprang up, as Saudi cities saw incredible growth in both population and infrastructure.

Sometimes a television monitor is brought into the classroom so that a male teacher can teach the class without having direct contact with his female students. This method is not as common today, however, because it makes communication between teachers and students difficult.

In the past Saudi education emphasized memorization. Students devoted most of their time to listening to, absorbing, and repeating the information teachers presented, limiting in-class activities and group work. Today this is changing. Most schools across the nation have science laboratories and plenty of computers. Students have greater opportunities to take more hands-on approaches to learning.

Class sizes in Saudi Arabia are small, and each student receives individualized attention. According to the Saudi Ministry of Education, the government agency in charge of education, there is an average of one teacher for every 15 students. This makes the kingdom's teacher-to-student ratio one of the lowest in the world.

Governments across the globe have tried to find ways to afford smaller class sizes, because studies show that lower teacher-to-student ratios result in greater learning. Because of Saudi Arabia's oil wealth and commitment to education, the country has achieved what so many countries have failed to accomplish.

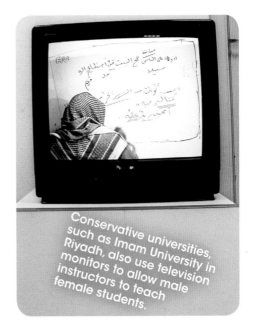

Conservative universities, such as Imam University in Riyadh, also use television monitors to allow male instructors to teach female students.

A Uniform Curriculum

The Ministry of Education sets the curriculum, dictating which classes students take. As a result, all students in a particular grade level across the country study the same subjects and take the same classes.

While school leaders are working to somewhat reform the curriculum, it remains geared toward religious studies and the sciences, with the arts receiving less emphasis. Students in intermediate school generally take around eight hours of religious study each week, more than any other subject. In addition, students study Arabic literature, English, math, science, social studies, and art. All students also take physical education classes, and female students take

An Average Day

The average school day begins with the national anthem and a reading from the Qur'an. Classes follow, usually with the more demanding subjects first, such as science or math. The day continues with between five and eight 45-minute class periods, sometimes ending with lighter classes such as art or computers.

In some schools, students receive just enough time between classes to walk from one room to the next. In other schools, students remain in the same room and at the same desk all day while the teachers move from room to room. Usually, students receive two breaks during their school day.

home skills classes, learning things like sewing and cooking.

Though high school students still have virtually no say in what classes they take, they are placed in one of two curriculum tracks, based on their interests: the literature track or the science track. Students enrolled in each track take the same subjects each day. But the total amount of time spent in these classes each week varies according to which track the student pursues.

When the school day ends, homework begins. Saudi middle school and high school students have homework almost every night during the school year. Many students spend from one to five hours each day studying and doing homework, depending on the student's commitment to success.

Generally students take exams at least twice a year. These tests cover the general curriculum areas and help determine if a student will move from one grade to the next. The week or two before exams are often very stressful for students. Many spend long evenings poring over notes and textbooks.

The first major exams usually take place in January at the end of the first semester. The second exams take place at the end of the second semester in late May or early June. The second exams also mark the end of the school year and the beginning of the much-anticipated three-month summer vacation.

Lower teacher-to-student ratios allow for more personalized teaching and attention.

Extracurricular Activities

Saudi schools emphasize extracurricular activities, including sports and a variety of other clubs. In general, boys have more extracurricular options. Boys' schools, for instance, are more likely to boast large soccer fields, basketball courts, and swimming pools for student sport teams.

Students can also join clubs. Calligraphy clubs are popular in Saudi Arabia, and many of the country's larger schools have theaters where student groups can perform in plays and concerts.

Educators hope that sports teams and clubs will help students remain interested in their education and school life. Holding student interest is important to the government leaders and school officials, who know that the nation's future success relies on the preparedness and skills of its current students. Fahd bin Abdul Aziz, former Saudi Arabian king, confirmed this commitment by saying,

"All our objectives in setting out to achieve the goals of an advanced society will not be fulfilled unless illiteracy is abolished throughout the land. We consider this one of the most important duties and responsibilities of ruling."

In the southern city of Najran, buildings are often made from mud and straw.

2 The Modern & the Traditional

A SAUDI TEENAGE BOY LIVING IN RIYADH, the kingdom's capital and one of its largest and most modern cities, can look out the window of his family's high-rise apartment and gaze upon a busy scene. He sees cars of all colors, makes, and sizes in bumper-to-bumper traffic, skyscrapers stretching into the clouds, huge supermarkets and shopping centers, and the famous McDonald's arches.

Miles away, a Saudi boy of the same age can step out of his family's large canvas tent and feel the hot desert sand on his bare feet. He sees nothing but miles of sand and hears only the sounds of his family's herd of sheep.

These two young men represent the two very different lifestyles that exist in Saudi Arabia: the modern life of the glittering big city and the traditional life of the Bedouin, or desert nomad.

21

Some Bedouins use hair from black goats to make wool tents, which are called Bait Al-Sha'ar, or "House of Hair."

The Bedouin Life

It is not known exactly how many people in Saudi Arabia live as Bedouins, which in Arabic means "nomad." But it is estimated that Bedouins account for less than 10 percent of the country's population. And that percentage is rapidly decreasing each year. Though the way of life is rare, Bedouin families can still be seen roaming the desert, raising and herding livestock.

Teens living the Bedouin lifestyle reside in large tents with their families. Together, they work as goat, camel, or sheep herders. The families do not have a fixed place they call home. Instead, they set up camp wherever they find good grazing land for the animals, and then, when needed, they pack up and travel through the desert to find fresh areas of grassland.

Bedouin teens usually have certain

duties they do each day. The boys typically have a great deal of responsibility,
helping take care of the animals and
providing for the family. The girls help
out by cooking, taking care of small
children, and, when needed, tending to
the animals.

Despite their desolate location, the
Bedouins have allowed some amenities of modern Arabia to seep into their
way of life. Today many Bedouins have
traded in their camels for foreign-made
pickup trucks and four-wheelers, and

Desert Hospitality

Amenities such as cell phones have modernized the lifestyles of Bedouins throughout the Middle East.

Though most Saudi families
have made the transition from
desert nomads to settled city folk,
many rituals and values of the
country's nomadic past are still
practiced. One of these lasting
characteristics is the value placed
on hospitality. Because water and
food are scarce in deserts, the
nomadic people have always
helped others in need—a tradition
that is carried on today. Saudis
pride themselves on treating their
guests well. The host, for example,
gives the visitor the best pieces of
meat and makes sure his guest's
plate and cup are never empty.

Saudi Arabia
Population Density and Political Map

Population Density
(People per square km)

- 25–100
- 10–24
- 1–10
- Fewer than 1
- Uninhabited

ISRAEL
JORDAN
EGYPT
IRAQ
KUWAIT
Persian Gulf
BAHRAIN
QATAR
UNITED ARAB EMIRATES
OMAN
YEMEN

Red Sea

Tabuk
Ha'il
Buraydah
Dammam
Al Mubarraz
Al Hufuf
Medina
Riyadh
Jeddah
Mecca
Taif
Khamis Mushayt
Najran
Farasan Islands

N
W E
S

0   100   200 mi.
0   100   200 km

their animal-hide tents for ones made of canvas. The Bedouin lifestyle is slowly dying out in Saudi Arabia as the desert nomads are forced to find work in the cities in order to provide for their families.

City Life

Less than 50 years ago, the majority of the Saudi population lived as Bedouins. But in a matter of decades, the country has transformed into a nation with an overwhelmingly urban population. Today, 80 percent of Saudi Arabia's 27 million people live in medium- to large-size urban areas.

Saudi Arabia has a number of highly populated cities. In Riyadh, for example, the population has grown from nearly 170,000 in 1970 to more than 4 million in 2006. That's more than the populations of Los Angeles, Paris, France, or Beirut, Lebanon.

Daily life for the Saudi teenager living in the big city is quite different from that of the Bedouin teen. The cities boast modern shopping malls filled with expensive Western fashions,

In Riyadh, where temperatures can reach 110 degrees Fahrenheit (43 degrees Celsius), private swimming pools provide welcomed relief.

grocery stores full of imported foods, and modern clinics and schools. These teens have all the features of modern living the Bedouins go without, including indoor plumbing, modern appliances, and air conditioning.

Instead of tents, urban teenagers and their families live in apartment buildings, single-family homes, or large compounds with their extended families. Many homes have swimming pools and beautiful gardens where teenagers can spend time outdoors. Almost every home in Saudi Arabia has a 7- to 9-foot (11- to 14-meter) wall around the yard to protect the family's privacy. A Saudi teen wanting even more

privacy can head off to his or her bedroom, a room some have to themselves and others share with siblings.

While their Bedouin counterparts spend a great deal of time helping with chores, most city teenagers have few

Major Cities

City	Population
Riyadh	4,328,067
Jeddah	2,934,584
Mecca	1,353,480
Medina	975,218
Dammam	793,553
Taif	540,437

*Source: World Gazetteer (2006 population estimates)

everyday chores and responsibilities. They are rarely asked to help wash the dishes, set the table, vacuum the floors, or take out the garbage. In this era of wealth and luxury, many Saudi families, even those in the middle class, employ household servants to do those jobs.

It is estimated that nearly 1 million foreign household servants work in homes throughout Saudi Arabia, and the average family has at least one servant to help with the day-to-day household duties. A news article in the *Arab News*, Saudi Arabia's English-language newspaper, reported that a number of Saudi families are so dependent on their domestic help that many teens do not even know how to do these tasks:

"Many Saudis never do a single household chore, and some would not be able to tell you where to find the cleaning detergents and cleaning equipment in their own homes."

In wealthy families, teenagers may even have their own servants. Instead of asking Mom or Dad for a ride to a friend's house, Saudi teens might ask a servant. And instead of parents helping them get ready for school in the morning, these teens

Without the responsibilities of household chores, Saudi teens are likely to spend their time at home hanging out with friends and family members.

The Five Pillars of Islam

According to the Qur'an, all Muslims are asked to fulfill five obligations called the Five Pillars of Islam:

1. **Declaration of belief**—To fulfill this requirement, a Muslim must make and believe the following statement: "There is no god but God, and Muhammad is his Messenger."

2. **Prayer**—Five times each day, Muslims must face Mecca and pray.

3. **Charity**—A Muslim is required to give to the poor if he or she is able.

4. **Fasting**—During the monthlong religious observance of Ramadan, a Muslim cannot eat or drink during daylight hours.

5. **Pilgrimage**—If they have the economic resources, Muslims must perform the Hajj, which is a pilgrimage to Mecca, at least once during their adulthood.

may have a servant making them breakfast and rushing them off to class. For many Saudi teens, domestic helpers have become vital figures in their daily lives.

Religion & Everyday Life

Life for the urban teenager is full of contrasts. While the teen has all the modern comforts, variety, and luxuries afforded by the wealth of the nation, daily activities still revolve around a traditional religious culture.

Central to the daily routine of all Saudis is the Islamic prayer cycle.

Religious Police

Anyone caught breaking the country's religious laws could suffer punishment from the kingdom's religious police, called the *mutawain*. They are also referred to as the Committee for the Propagation of Virtue and the Prevention of Vice. These religious officers patrol the streets and monitor public places. They look for people breaking the separation of the sexes laws, women who are not properly covered in public, or anyone under the influence of drugs or alcohol. Though it rarely happens, the mutawain, who are always male, can use a cane to strike a person who does not follow the rules. Normally, though, the officers just reprimand lawbreakers verbally.

mutawain
MUT-ah-wane

Devout Muslims stop all daily activities and pray five times a day—at sunrise, midday, afternoon, sunset, and night. During prayer times, every shop in the city closes, so everyone can participate in prayers. The people pray either at home, school, local mosques, or even in the streets if needed. To pray, Muslims kneel on the ground and face the holy city of Mecca.

This cycle of prayer is not limited to Saudi Arabians; Muslims worldwide are expected to kneel, face Mecca,

Businesses, like the Saudi Lighting factory, often provide employees with a special room for prayer times.

The daily prayer ritual involves specific body placement, ranging from standing to kneeling with the head on the ground.

and pray five times each day. In Saudi Arabia, though, the prayer times are required by law, and the religious police can punish anyone caught not performing the ritual.

The Saudi teenager's average day begins with prayer. After prayer, the teenager usually has about one or two hours before school. During this time, he or she might do homework or take a quick nap. Breakfast is the first meal of the day, usually eaten before heading off to school at around 6:30 A.M. The second prayer time begins around 11:30 A.M., after which most Saudis eat lunch and then resume school. After

school, the teenagers usually return home and have free time to do as they please. Dinner is served between 7 and 10 P.M., and many teens go to bed between 9 P.M. and 1 A.M. All evening activities, though, are interrupted with the sunset and nighttime prayers.

Food & Drink

Saudis generally eat three meals a day: one in the morning, one around noon, and one in the evening. Popular foods and drinks are tied to the country's desert environment and nomadic heritage. Many traditional Saudi meals include meat from animals that could

Saudi men and boys feast on a dish consisting of baby camel, roasted whole and surrounded by rice.

survive the harsh desert climate, mainly goats, lambs, or camels. In both Bedouin and urban settings, almost every meal is served with *khubz*, which is an Arabian flatbread. Many Saudi Arabian meals also include dates.

Saudis usually eat these sweet fruits, most of which are grown in the kingdom's eastern Al-Hasa region, as an appetizer or a dessert.

khubz
kuhbs

THE MODERN & THE TRADITIONAL

If teenagers living in cities become tired of traditional meals, they can choose among a variety of restaurants, serving everything from American fast food to expensive French cuisine. Many teenagers enjoy Western food chains, such as McDonald's, Kentucky Fried Chicken, and Chili's. In fact, after school, a teenage boy can easily swing through the local Burger King, ordering a hamburger, fries, and a Pepsi for the ride home. Like teenagers across the globe, the

Traditional Meals

- *Kabsah*—camel, lamb, or chicken with rice and other ingredients

- *Falafel*—deep-fried chickpea balls flavored with garlic and herbs

- *Shawerma*—thinly sliced lamb or chicken rolled with pickles

- *Fuul*—a paste of fava beans, garlic, and lemon

kabsah
KEHB-sah

falafel
feh-LAH-fel

shawerma
sha-WEAR-ma

fuul
FOOL

Thanks to the growth of Middle Eastern restaurants, falafels are enjoyed around the world.

Many fast food restaurants use a segregation board to create separate ordering stations for men and women.

majority of Saudi teens love fast food and junk food.

Soda or sports drinks are common refreshment choices for Saudi teens. Popular traditional drinks include coffee and tea. Like most teens, young Saudis are not allowed to drink alcohol. In fact, everyone in the kingdom is forbidden from drinking alcohol, because Islam discourages alcohol consumption. Because Islamic rules are also Saudi law, anyone of any age caught drinking alcohol risks arrest and punishment by the nation's religious police.

The Red Sea is a popular place for family visits, and climbing along the rocks that line the coast is a favorite pastime.

3

The Importance of Family

IMAGINE LIVING IN A HOME WITH NOT ONLY YOUR PARENTS AND SIBLINGS, but your grandparents, aunts, uncles, cousins, nieces, and nephews. For a number of Saudi teens, such living conditions are the norm, and they enjoy and appreciate the arrangement.

Nothing is more importante to a person's identity than his or her family. Family determines how you spend your time and with whom you spend your time. Though teenagers in the kingdom often have friends outside the family, they spend a great deal of their time socializing inside the home.

The gated wall around a Saudi compound protects the home from the harsh desert winds and provides the family with privacy.

Close Family Ties

Because having a large family provides a sense of pride to a Saudi father, the average teenager has five or six brothers and sisters. This makes for a very active home!

To add to the family's excitement, as many as three or four generations of family members may live in the same home or compound. A family compound consists of a group of single-family homes, all of which are lived in by the extended family members. The homes are usually connected to each other and surrounded on all four sides by a huge wall.

In the last 20 years, family dynamics in Saudi Arabia have changed. Because of modernization and increased economic opportunity, more families today are deciding to live in single-family homes or city apartment buildings, instead of large family compounds. These modern homes often have contemporary Western furniture and living room areas that overflow with television sets, DVD players, and video game systems.

Despite the modern homes and new technologies, family still remains highly important. Saudi culture calls for teenagers to remain respectful to their extended family members and, most important, to their parents. Teens tend to follow the well-known proverb that teaches: "Heaven lies underneath the feet of the mother." They believe that the way to get to heaven is by respecting and honoring one's parents.

Because few people move away from the town where they were raised, teenagers often have special relation-

ships with their grandparents and other extended family members. If the family does not live in the same compound, Saudi teenagers and their families normally will travel at least once or twice a week to the home of their grandparents. Often aunts, uncles, and cousins will try to make the visit on the same day each week, so everyone can eat together, play together, and catch up on any family news. These weekly meetings help to keep family members close.

Of course, like in all cultures, there are some Saudi teens who do not appreciate the time with family. They would rather be hanging out with friends or playing video games. But in general, nearly all members of the

Expensive furniture and electronics afforded by the country's oil wealth changed the look of many Saudi homes.

Gender segregation limits the number of jobs for women in Saudi Arabia. They often choose to spend their days caring for their children and gathering with other women for tea.

younger generation treat their elderly grandparents with respect and admiration. In fact, Saudis consider it an honor to care for elderly relatives, and teenagers often do their part to help make their older relatives feel loved, respected, and appreciated. Like most grandparents worldwide, Saudi grandparents share stories of family history, passing tales from generation to generation.

Gender Roles in the Family

Saudi culture has been a patriarchal society since before the country's founding in the early 1900s, and emphasis on male dominance still holds strong today. The oldest male in the extended family, whether he is the father or brother, holds the title as the head of the family. Teenagers, children, and women are expected to remain submissive to the male authority in their lives. Women play important roles in the home, having a great deal of influence over the day-to-day activities. But in many families, they have a secondary position of power behind their fathers, husbands, and oftentimes, even their sons.

The family chain of command also affects relationships between siblings.

Behind the Wheel

Inequality between the sexes exists in the kingdom's laws. For example, women are not allowed to drive. For this reason, teenage males often fill much of their free time driving the women in their family around town.

After taking a driving exam, Saudi males receive a one-year permit at age 17, which does not require them to have an adult in the car. They receive an actual driver's license at 18. Despite legal driving ages, many rural Saudis begin driving as young as 10 or 12. Without police to enforce driving age limits, young Saudis and even women in rural areas drive as much as they please. Even in cities, young males often get behind the wheel without a license and take to the Saudi streets.

Many believe that the high number of young drivers on city roads has contributed to the country's frequent traffic accidents. Reckless driving and tragic accidents—resulting in an average of 12 deaths each day and four injuries every hour—have become all too common on Saudi streets. The government is in the process of passing new requirements to make the roadways safer for all drivers.

Conservative Saudis fear allowing women to drive would result in too much exposure to men outside the family.

Sons usually receive more freedom than daughters. For instance, Saudi families are more likely to allow their sons to go out of the home without a chaperone. When a male turns 17, legally he can drive a car, while his sisters cannot.

In more traditional families, the customary role of a daughter consists of helping take care of her brothers and other male relatives. She often receives less attention and affection from her parents than her brothers. However, this is beginning to change. Today a growing number of families are seeing their daughters as valuable individuals who deserve equal love and respect. As a result young women have been attaining more equality in their home lives.

Separation of the Sexes

In the past, Saudi rules about the separation of the sexes were much harsher. According to tradition, men and women of the same family were to live and eat in separate living quarters. So for centuries, all male family members over the age of 7 would reside in one area of the home, while the women and young children would live in another. This tradition, though, has changed in most of Saudi Arabia. Today most families move more freely throughout the home.

When guests visit, however, the family often segregates according to gender. For this reason, most homes have separate living room areas for men and women. Unrelated men and

In the privacy of family compounds, it is becoming more common for teens of both genders to hang out together.

السوم مخصص للعوائل فقط

Sorry for the inconvenience ...
Today is for families only

A Riyadh mall sets special times for women and families to shop. Young men are not allowed to enter alone at these times.

women do not have to worry about crossing each other's paths. Both living rooms usually have separate entrances and restrooms.

The separation of the sexes impacts teenagers and how they spend their time. For instance, if a young woman's father or brother has a friend in the home, she and the other women of the family usually remain out of sight. The same is true if the girl has a friend over to visit; she and her friend often must remain in certain areas of the home, away from male members of the family. However, the level to which the sexes are separated in a home varies greatly from family to family.

The separation between the sexes is less strict inside the home today, but the division remains strong in virtually all public spheres. The Qur'an remains the acting constitution in Saudi Arabia. According to the Saudi interpretation of the Qur'an, women and men not of the same immediate family should not directly interact. The separation of the sexes has much to do with the emphasis Islam places on modesty. The religion expects its followers, women especially, to remain reserved, wholesome, and humble.

To protect a woman's modesty in public, once a girl reaches puberty, some families will require her to be accompanied by a male relative when she heads to the mall, school, or any other public place. Most important, she is to steer clear of all unrelated men she passes on her way.

In addition, she is expected to keep her entire body covered when in the presence of men outside her family. While in public, all women, including foreign female visitors, wear loose-fitting black cloaks, called *abayas*, over their regular clothing. The abaya covers a woman from head-to-toe except her face. Many women also wear a black veil, called a *niqab*, over their faces in public.

In the Islamic world, Saudi Arabia's strict gender separation rules are extreme compared to most. For centuries, the Arabian culture has gone to great lengths to keep unrelated men and women apart. The Saudis' traditional tribal culture and unique interpretation of the Qur'an play huge roles in these gender ideals.

abaya
aa-BYE-uh

niqab
nee-KAAB

Social Lives

Because going into public remains somewhat of an inconvenience, and because family is so important in Saudi culture, most social activities for male and female teenagers take place in the home.

As a growing number of young people gain an education, more teenagers today create friendships outside the family circle. These friends, of course, are supposed to be members of the same sex.

Modern shopping malls provide a favorite hangout for Saudi youths.

Fashion Corner

Saudi male clothing is closely linked to desert life. Almost every day, men wear a loose-fitting, ankle-length shirt called a *thobe*, which is usually white. The garment's lightness and length are beneficial for Saudi Arabia's extremely warm and often windy climate. On their heads, Saudi males wear a *ghutra*, a headdress that is usually either white or red-and-white checkered. Saudis find the headdress handy because it can easily be pulled in front of the face during sandstorms.

Saudi female dress is closely linked to the Islamic emphasis on modesty. Women wear the abaya and the veil in public, partly because it keeps unrelated men from looking at them. It also gives each woman a sense of anonymity. Islam emphasizes equality among its citizens. When all women—and men, for that matter—dress alike, no one stands out and, in theory, no one can be judged according to social or economic status.

thobe
thohb

ghutra
GUH-trah

43

A couple looks out over Riyadh from Kingdom Tower, the country's tallest building. Public displays of affection are rare in the conservative country.

Single men and women who are past puberty are not supposed to have any social contact with the opposite sex. When friends spend time together, they usually hang out at one of their homes because Saudi towns and cities have few public places for them to meet. There are no movie theaters, skating rinks, or clubs.

In general, social dating is out of the question for Saudi teens. Most young men and women do not meet in the common Western fashion, where they date, fall in love, and then decide to marry. Instead, families play a big role in helping their children find a mate.

Because interaction between the sexes is restricted, a teenage boy

wanting to marry often depends on his female relatives to give him information about girls he might be interested in. When he decides which girl—or girls—he wants to pursue, he can speak with her family members about her. If the families are more modern, he might call her on the phone or even talk to her face-to-face in the presence of family. If marriage is proposed, the couple's families might meet and the two often go on a few chaperoned dates. At any point, either can reject the offer to marry.

The Grand Mosque in Mecca is designed to accommodate the millions of pilgrims who take part in a five-day pilgrimage known as the Hajj.

4

Celebrating in the Kingdom

THE LARGE ORANGE SUN SITS LOW IN THE DESERT SKY, with the last streaks of sunlight gleaming off the tall, gold towers of a local mosque. Filing out of the mosque, sets of fathers and sons have just finished saying evening prayers together. Red sand blows across the city's streets as the men and their sons head toward their homes. These streets, usually packed with pedestrians and cars, are silent during this time of prayer. As usual, all shops, restaurants, and corporations are closed, but this particular day is special.

It is Ramadan, Saudi Arabia's most important holiday. During the month-long celebration, everyone is expected to be especially observant of the prayer times and to reaffirm his or her religious devotion.

Ramadan: A Time for Praying & Fasting

Ramadan takes place during the ninth lunar month of Islam's official calendar—the Hijrah calendar. The holiday is a time of great rejoicing for teenagers. But Saudi Arabia does not celebrate its holidays with parties, parades, or carnivals. Instead, people see Ramadan and other Saudi holidays as times to concentrate on building stronger relationships with God.

Throughout Ramadan, Islamic law requires Muslims who have reached puberty and beyond to fast during daylight hours, meaning they do not eat or drink until after dark.

Some schools close for the month, while others hold classes in the early morning and late afternoon, sending students home to rest in between sessions. Families sleep as much as possible during the day, then hang out together during the nighttime. In fact, one of the more exciting parts of Ramadan are the large family meals that often take place after sunset and before sunrise. The odd mealtimes usually result in a festive atmosphere of lively chatter and laughter.

The Hijrah Calendar

The Hijrah calendar, the official calendar of Saudi Arabia and Islam, consists of 354 days and is divided into 12 lunar months. Each month begins with the sighting of the new moon. Once a new moon appears, a new month begins, and that month does not end until the next new moon is sighted. People can estimate with high accuracy when a new moon will be seen, but no one can know for sure. While each month still consists of about 29 or 30 days, an established calendar does not exist in Saudi Arabia.

The 12 months of the Islamic calendar are:

Muharram
Safar
Rabi'a al-Awal
Rabi'a ath-Thani
Jumada al-Ula
Jamada Ath-Thani
Rajab
Sha'aban
Ramadan
Shawwal
Dhul Qa'dah
Dhul Hijjah

During Eid al-Fitr, the mosques overflow with people for morning prayer. Some are left to pray on the streets instead.

Celebrating the Feasts

After 29 or 30 days of eating and drinking only between sunset and sunrise, Saudi Arabians celebrate the end of Ramadan with Eid al-Fitr. During this three-day national holiday, all schools and businesses close. Families pray together, visit friends, play games, and eat.

The first day of Eid al-Fitr usually is the most festive. In the morning and the evening, families hold large celebratory meals, and loved ones often exchange gifts.

Many people also see Eid al-Fitr as a time for forgiveness. Muslims are encouraged to settle all differences and disagreements with others during this holiday. For this reason, Eid al-Fitr provides an excellent opportunity for

The traditional Eid al-Fitr meal is a roasted lamb stuffed with saffron rice, nuts, and spices.

squabbling teen siblings to put an end to their fighting and forgive past actions.

The only other national holiday celebrated in Saudi Arabia is Eid al-Adha, or the "feast of the sacrifice." The holiday falls on the 10th of Dhul Hijjah, which is the final month of the Islamic year. Like Eid al-Fitr, this is a time of great feasting and socializing.

On the morning of this holiday, each family sacrifices an animal. They may butcher a goat, lamb, or pigeon, depending on the family's wealth. Then extended family members usually gather together to share a meal. Sticking to tradition, most families donate a portion of the meat to the poor.

On Eid al-Adha, Muslims across the world remember the prophet Abraham. According to the Qur'an, nearly 4,000 years ago God asked Abraham to sacrifice his son to prove his religious devotion. But right before the sacrifice took place, God commanded Abraham to sacrifice a ram instead. On Eid al-Adha, Muslims celebrate Abraham's loyalty to God and his willingness to follow God's orders.

Like all other aspects of Saudi life, most holidays and celebrations revolve around Islam. In the kingdom, few people throw birthday parties, special anniversary dinners, or even independence day get-togethers. And because other religions cannot be practiced openly in Saudi Arabia, Christian holidays such as Christmas and Easter or Jewish holidays such as Hanukkah are not celebrated publicly.

Saudi shepherds sell many sheep for Eid al-Adha. Families sacrifice the animals in remembrance of Abraham's willingness to sacrifice his son to God.

The Hajj

The Ka'ba, at the center of the Grand Mosque, is covered with a black silk cloth.

If they can afford it, all Muslims are supposed to journey to the holy city of Mecca at least once in their lives during the Eid al-Adha holiday. This pilgrimage is called the Hajj, and it starts around the seventh or eighth of the month of Dhul Hijjah and lasts about five days. Each year, approximately 2.5 million Muslims from across the world travel to Saudi Arabia to take part. In Islam, the pilgrimage is one of the chief duties assigned by God, and its completion is a major milestone in the life of a Muslim.

For centuries, people made this trip through the desert on camelback. Today the primary form of transportation used by Hajj pilgrims is air travel. Most pilgrims from around the world and throughout Saudi Arabia fly into Jeddah's enormous modern airport, located about 45 miles (72 km) from Mecca. There is even a special Hajj terminal for pilgrims. From the airport, pilgrims board huge buses that take them to the outskirts of Mecca, where they begin their preparation rituals.

In addition to being the place where God gave Muhammad the verses of the Qur'an, Mecca is home to the Grand Mosque. Five times a day, millions of Muslims face Mecca to pray because Muslims consider the Grand Mosque the spiritual center of their religion. A large, black, cube-shaped shrine known as the Ka'ba is the heart of the Grand Mosque. Embedded in the Ka'ba is a black stone that holds special religious significance for Muslims, who believe the stone was sent from heaven.

During the Hajj, pilgrims follow Muhammad's teachings and perform certain acts that are symbolic of the lives of Abraham and his family. They take part in several rituals and ceremonies that help cleanse them of sin and reaffirm their religious devotion. The events include many days of intense prayer and reflection. On the ninth day, the pilgrims travel to the Plain of Arafat, an area near Mecca where Muhammad gave his farewell sermon. There they pray standing up from noon to sundown.

The Hajj ends with the Eid al-Adha sacrifice and feast. The Saudi government provides more than 1 million animals to sacrifice for the Eid al-Adha celebration. Any remaining meat is given to the poor in Asia, Africa, and elsewhere. Once the feast is over, the pilgrims have successfully completed the Hajj with a new sense of peace and goodness.

Honoring Life's Big Moments

While they celebrate few national holidays, the people of this desert country do honor significant moments in people's lives. Saudis often celebrate the major steps of life that show personal growth and maturity. When someone marries, gives birth, or dies, Saudis mark those events with special care and respect.

Weddings, for example, celebrate a person's transition from adolescence to adulthood. In Saudi Arabia, teens are considered of age for marriage as soon as they hit puberty. On average, females marry between the ages of 16 and 18, while males marry between the ages 16 and 20. In rural areas some girls marry as young as 10 years old, though it is very rare. In urban areas women tend to marry older, in their 20s, because many choose to pursue higher education. Marriage remains an important rite of passage for Saudi teens, showing an individual's readiness to take on larger responsibilities and family duties.

To honor this important stage, Saudis throw large wedding parties with lots of guests, food, and entertainment. The bride's family usually spares no expense when planning for the big event. Typically, Saudi weddings occur in the evenings at the bride's home or in elaborate local buildings that hold large crowds.

If the family is wealthy, large lush gardens and backyards may serve as

An elaborate hall is the men's gathering place for a wealthy family's wedding celebration.

Men celebrate a new marriage with traditional dances. Photographs of the women's celebration are rare because of privacy restrictions.

the backdrop for the wedding celebration. The scent of garden flowers mixes with the alluring aroma of the 40 to 50 freshly cooked lambs that will be the main meal for countless guests. According to tradition, the sounds of drums rumble through the scene to signify the beginning of the celebration, and later to announce the appearance of the bride.

Unlike weddings in most countries, Saudi weddings basically are female affairs. At traditional Saudi weddings, the groom and the bride's father are the only men who attend the large celebration, and they usually do not stay long. The two men hurry off to meet the other male family members, who often get

together at a separate location to enjoy a more subdued gathering. According to David E. Long, a former U.S. Foreign Service officer in Saudi Arabia, "The women's party is much more elaborate and undoubtedly more fun."

Because of this, teen girls look forward to these opportunities to socialize outside their own homes without wearing the abaya and veil. It is a rare chance for girls to show off their fancy jewelry and expensive bright-colored dresses.

Soon after marriage, the couple is expected to start a family. Births in Saudi Arabia are events of great celebration, especially if the baby is a boy. Sons provide a sense of pride to the father, so giving birth to a son is one of a woman's

What's in a Name?

Generally, a male Saudi's paternal ancestry can be traced through his name. For instance, if Sattam has a son named Salman, his son will be known as Salman ibn Sattam, which in Arabic means "Salman son of Sattam." The names of many Saudis can go back as many as four generations. The official name of Saudi Arabia's founder and first king was Abdul Aziz bin Abdul Rahman ibn Faisal al Saud. Rather than taking their husband's name, women in Saudi Arabia keep their father's family name throughout their lives, even after they marry.

primary life achievements. Traditionally, the birth of a daughter brought sadness and shame to a Saudi family, but today, more families are seeing the advantages and joys of female children. Whether the child is a boy or a girl, large birthday celebrations are strongly discouraged.

Returning to the Earth

Elaborate funerals also rarely take place in the kingdom, yet people do honor the dead in their own unique ways. When a person dies, the relatives, teenagers included, wash and prepare the body according to tradition. Females prepare the body of female relatives, while males do the washing for other males.

Once the washing rituals are complete, further preparations are handed over to male relatives. The men, young and old, prepare for the desert burial. Regular cemeteries do not exist in the kingdom. Instead, men bring the body into the vast Arabian desert and bury their loved one in the sand, usually without even a gravestone to mark the burial spot. The dead in Saudi Arabia are welcomed back into the earth, and the people left behind trust that they will see their loved ones again in heaven.

Death is not viewed as an ending, but as a new beginning. When people die, they move to a more peaceful place. Saudis believe they will be rewarded in death for the strict religious life they lived on Earth, so death marks the end of the life cycle, and the first step toward a new life in heaven.

Burying a King

Funerals are kept simple, even for the most powerful members of Saudi society. When the country's former king, King Fahd, died on August 1, 2005, his body was wrapped in a plain brown shroud, and his male relatives, along with general citizens, carried his body into the desert on a thin, wooden board. Abiding with Muslim custom, they buried the king in an unidentified grave in the desert near Riyadh.

Mourners at King Fahd's burial chanted "Allahu akbar," or "God is great."

Saudi men work in the traders room of a bank in Riyadh. The Saudi stock market is the largest market in the Arab world.

5

Higher Education & the Workforce

FEW SAUDI TEENS WORK DURING HIGH SCHOOL, with the exception of those who help out on the family farm or in the family business. The majority of Saudis enter the workforce for the very first time when they graduate from high school. But even after high school, many young people concentrate on their studies at college, delaying their entrance into the workforce for a few more years.

Today, Saudis have more options than ever when it comes to higher education. Like secondary education, or high school, post-secondary education is a relatively new phenomenon in the kingdom. The first university was not founded until 1957. In the past, most Saudis seeking a college degree had to travel out of the country to attend universities in countries like Egypt, England, and the United States.

59

Founded in 1957, King Saud University in Riyadh is the kingdom's oldest university.

While nearly 16,000 Saudi Arabians still choose to study abroad, around 200,000 Saudi students have opted to attend universities in their homeland. Currently eight major universities span the desert nation, offering higher education to any Saudi wanting a degree.

Government Support

The Saudi government offers incredible opportunities for young people wanting to attend local universities and colleges. One of the many advantages of Saudi Arabia's vast oil wealth has been the government's ability to make higher education accessible to all young people in the kingdom.

University study is free for Saudi citizens, and in many instances, the government even supplies college students with money to pay for living expenses. This way, most students do not have to work while in college, allowing them to give all their attention to their studies. And Saudi grads can enter the working world free from the debt of student loans.

In the past, the Saudi government handed out substantial financial aid to students wishing to study abroad as well. However, with the recent construction of new universities, colleges, and vocational schools throughout the kingdom, the government has been able to limit the amount of support it gives to students studying in other countries.

Like most universities across the world, Saudi universities tend to be large campuses with countless

Imam University in Riyadh features a separate campus for women.

services and facilities for students. Most universities offer student dormitories. Of course, the university administration keeps the dorms separated according to gender, so male and female students do not mix.

Five of the country's eight major universities admit both men and women, and each year about the same number of men and women graduate from Saudi universities. Women take separate classes and use separate facilities from male students. Sometimes campuses have "women-only" hours in places like the library or the lunchroom to avoid the expense of building double facilities to keep the genders separate.

Despite the segregation, female students basically receive the same education as males. Plans are under way to construct the nation's first women's

Saudi Soldiers

Another option for male Saudi teenagers once they graduate from high school is to join the military. Today an increasing number of young men enlist in the armed forces, making the Saudi military one of the most rapidly growing in the world. The armed forces consist of an army, navy, air force, air defense force, and national guard. All members of the military are volunteers. The government does not allow women to serve in the military.

university. The facility, which is to be built in Riyadh, could change the way women experience university study.

Current Saudi students can choose from a wide variety of academic areas upon entering the nation's universities. Many of the universities offer degrees in medicine, and some operate large university hospitals.

Not surprisingly, strong religious upbringings lead many Saudi teens to choose religion as their area of study. In fact, it is estimated that more than 15 percent of Saudi university students enroll in a curriculum based on Islamic studies. Many of the male religion graduates hope to work as clerics in local mosques.

Popular College Majors

Arabic
Business
Denistry
Education
Engineering
Geography
History
Medicine
Pharmacology
Religion
Science

Where's My Job?

Universities are releasing newly educated people into the workforce by the thousands each year, yet many of these young people remain unemployed. An estimated 25 percent of Saudi citizens do not have jobs. The lack of available jobs has produced a large number of young people who are dissatisfied with their limited options and uncertain futures.

The enormous foreign workforce in Saudi Arabia is a major contributor to this substantial unemployment problem.

Foreign workers bring support to a variety of industries, including residential building.

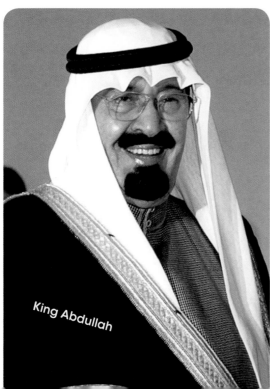

King Abdullah

It is estimated that about 70 percent of Saudi Arabia's entire workforce consists of workers from foreign countries. A large number of these foreign workers came to the country during the oil boom in the late 1970s to help with development and modernization. Today, foreign employees hold positions in all levels of the workforce, including doctors, business leaders, and teachers, while others work as maids, manufacturers, and carpenters.

One reason why foreign workers have flourished in the kingdom for decades is because of the Saudi attitude toward work. The jobs available are in areas such as manufacturing and construction—areas of employment looked down upon by Saudi culture since the oil boom. The oil wealth created a new generation of Saudis who tend to consider doing manual labor dishonorable. Because honor and pride are extremely important to Saudis, this attitude toward work has played a key role in the high unemployment rates.

For the past few years, the Saudi royal family has spent a great deal of time trying to develop solutions to the country's unemployment problems. In 2005, King Abdullah said the unemployment problem had improved in recent years, but the country still had work to do:

"We need to find approximately 100,000 jobs for those who are seeking jobs but cannot find them at this time."

Saudi leaders feel great pride for their vocational schools and invited Prince Charles of England to visit one during a 2006 trip.

The country wants to create more career options for Saudi nationals, and the government has even offered extra financial support to companies that hire primarily Saudi workers.

To help Saudis find more pride in skilled labor, the government has supported the construction of more vocational schools. These institutions prepare young people for highly skilled positions—electricians, carpenters, mechanics, and machinists—necessary for a modern industrial society. These schools are a fundamental part of the country's plan to phase out foreign workers and train Saudis to take over the many jobs currently filled by the huge foreign workforce.

Before modernization, Saudi Arabia had little need for people skilled in technical and industrial fields.

Division of Labor

Agriculture	Industry	Services
3.3%	61.3%	35.4%

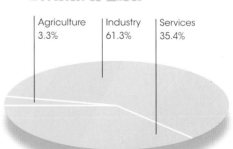

Source: United States Central Intelligence Agency. *The World Factbook—Saudi Arabia.*

But today those are exactly the kinds of workers they need! As a result, a growing number of teenagers choose these technical options as opposed to university studies. By building more vocational schools throughout the country, the kingdom has begun to work toward producing more employable citizens.

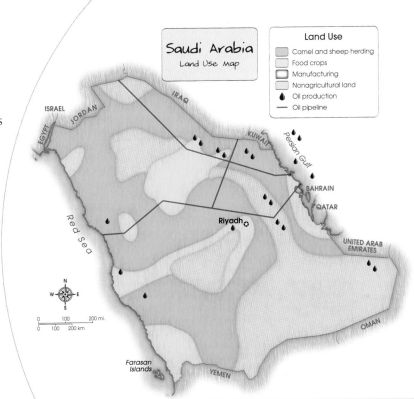

Saudi Arabia
Land Use Map

Land Use
- Camel and sheep herding
- Food crops
- Manufacturing
- Nonagricultural land
- ◆ Oil production
- — Oil pipeline

ISRAEL
JORDAN
EGYPT
IRAQ
KUWAIT
Persian Gulf
BAHRAIN
QATAR
Riyadh
UNITED ARAB EMIRATES
Red Sea
OMAN
Farasan Islands
YEMEN

0   100   200 mi.
0   100   200 km

The Saudi Workweek

It is typical in Middle Eastern countries for the workweek to begin on Saturday and end on Wednesday. Friday is the Islamic Sabbath, and all male citizens are required to attend a noon service at one of a city's major mosques. Very few businesses open at all on that day. Businesses also close every day at the Islamic prayer times. Most banks and private businesses open in the morning between 7 and 8 and remain open until around noon. Then at noon, the businesses close for prayer until about 3 P.M. and reopen until about 6 P.M. During the afternoon hours off, workers often pray, have lunch, and maybe even take a quick nap.

Keeping It in the Family

The Saudi students who have little to worry about when it comes to job searching are the ones with family connections to a particular business. Most businesses in the country are owned and controlled by families and tend to hire people close to the family. So if a teenage boy works in his father's grocery store or at his uncle's contracting business, he likely works shoulder-to-shoulder with his brothers, grandfather, cousins, and uncles.

The majority of the urban teens who enter the workforce will most likely be employed in service or industry jobs. The service sector employs 35 percent of the workforce. Retail employs the most service workers. Along with small family-owned retail stores, many people

In 2004, the Saudi government banned foreign workers in gold and jewelry shops in an attempt to ensure jobs for nationals.

Fruit and vegetable crops, such as tomatoes, are consumed almost completely by Saudis, leaving little for export to neighboring countries.

work in the large shopping centers and malls.

Industry and manufacturing jobs employ the most workers—about 61 percent of the workforce. The majority of the manufacturing jobs are tied to oil production, but Saudis also find employment manufacturing products like cement and steel.

Another group of teenagers who often take over the family business are rural teens. About 12 percent of working Saudis are employed in agricultural-related fields. Though water is scarce in the region, Saudi farmers grow produce such as wheat, dates, potatoes, and watermelon. Like farmers in other nations, Saudi farmers teach their children the farming trade, in hopes that they will take over the family farm.

Also, the Bedouins' lifestyle has been passed on through hundreds of generations and is still being passed on today. Bedouin teenagers often choose to remain close to their family and continue the nomadic way of life.

Eight local soccer teams compete in the annual Beach Soccer Championship tournament, which was first held in 2003.

6

Free Time in a Desert Country

LIKE OTHER PARTS OF THEIR DAY, Saudi teens' free time is filled with a blend of modern and traditional activities. One day, a teenage girl might be practicing ancient Bedouin dances, reciting passages from the Qur'an, and making beautiful Bedouin jewelry. The next day, she might spend the afternoon surfing Internet chat rooms, watching reruns of the American sitcom Friends, and shopping with pals in one of the city's shopping plazas.

Other favorite pastimes include hanging out at a local coffeeshop, spending time at the beach, and participating in sports such as soccer or volleyball.

Crafter's Corner

The creation of exquisite handmade crafts has been a tradition in the kingdom since ancient times. Today members of the older generation pass these traditions on to Saudi youth, hoping to keep the art forms alive.

Bedouins have been decorating jewelry with stunning pieces of coral, turquoise, and pearls for centuries. Some of the most popular pieces of their jewelry have been the triangular and crescent-shaped creations. Bedouins often wore them to ward off the "evil eye," which traditional Bedouins thought to be a look given that would bring harm to another person.

Another esteemed traditional craft is calligraphy. Saudis value the art of creating beautifully written Arabic letters. Calligraphers often will copy quotes from the Qur'an onto the sides of buildings or canvases.

Fun in the Sun & Sand

In a country without movie theaters, nightclubs, or dance parties, one thing is for sure: Saudi teens have to be creative when it comes to filling their free time. Young people have found ways to make the empty, often very hot

While sharing a desert picnic with her cousins, 16-year-old Madawy turns away and covers her face after a carload of boys comes across the group. The action is meant to protect her modesty.

deserts places of excitement. Desert picnics and drives are a popular form of entertainment. Families will sometimes take an afternoon to drive—in an air-conditioned car, of course—through the desert, to enjoy the scenery and look for wildlife, such as baboons and gazelles.

These drives have become popular among teenage boys as well. It is not uncommon to see a car with two or three teenagers traveling down desert roads, which are raised to prevent sand from building up on the road-way. These boys rarely have an actual destination. They are driving purely for recreational purposes.

While Saudi Arabia is mainly a desert country, it also contains some of the most beautiful beaches and coastlines in the world. The country is bordered by the Red Sea to the west and the Persian Gulf to the east. Many of the kingdom's largest and most industrialized cities are along these two coastlines.

For teenagers living in coastal cities like Jeddah or Dammam, few recreational alternatives can compete with spending an afternoon at the beach. Because unrelated men and women cannot mix, there are separate beaches for single men and for women and families. Groups of teen boys often replace their customary thobes with shorts and wade in the salty waters of the sea. Many also enjoy water sports like waterskiing, windsurfing, and sailing.

Young women also enjoy the beaches. In modern cities and villages, groups of teenage girls might hang out at the beach together without a chaperone if their families will allow it.

It is common to see beaches speckled with the black abayas of Saudi teen girls and women.

Hot Spots

For Saudis, the cities of Jeddah and Taif, both located on the kingdom's western edge, are popular vacation destinations. Jeddah is Saudi Arabia's most modern city. Families from throughout Saudi Arabia travel there for its beautiful beaches, museums, sports complexes, shopping centers, and amazing mosques.

Taif is a city of about 500,000 people, but during the summer months, the population nearly doubles with

visitors who swarm there to escape the country's extreme heat. Tucked away in the western mountains, the city generally has one of the most pleasant climates in all of Saudi Arabia. Because of its beautiful scenery, fresh mountain air, and relatively cool temperatures, even the royal family makes this city its summer home.

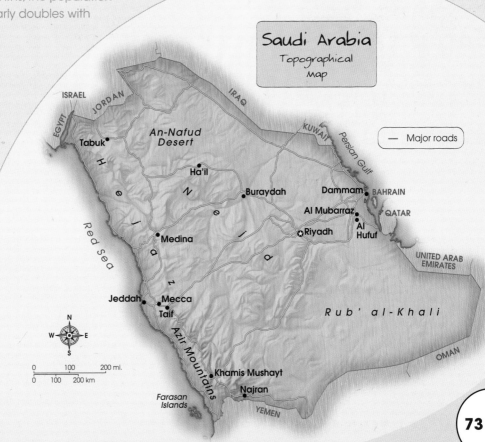

Saudi Arabia
Topographical Map

— Major roads

ISRAEL
JORDAN
EGYPT
IRAQ
KUWAIT
Persian Gulf
Tabuk
An-Nafud Desert
Ha'il
Buraydah
Dammam
BAHRAIN
Al Mubarraz
QATAR
Riyadh
Al Hufuf
Medina
Red Sea
UNITED ARAB EMIRATES
Rub' al-Khali
Jeddah
Mecca
Taif
Asir Mountains
OMAN
Khamis Mushayt
Najran
Farasan Islands
YEMEN

N W E S

0   100   200 mi.
0 100 200 km

Between 20,000 and 30,000 spectators watch the annual camel race.

In more traditional areas, however, girls have to convince their parents or brothers to spend the afternoon at the beach as well. The same rules concerning public dress apply for women at the beach, but their long, black abayas do not stop many of them from wading and swimming in the water—abayas and all!

Sports: Mixing the Traditional & the Modern

Sporting events are another way that young Saudi Arabians fill their time. Sports have been important on the Arabian Peninsula for centuries, and today, all young people in the kingdom are encouraged to join athletic programs either through school or their community. Traditionally, camel races and horse races have been the most popular sports. The Arabian horse has a reputation for being extremely fast, and though they may not look like it, camels are quite speedy as well. An Arabian camel can trot at a pace of about 10 miles (16 kilometers) an hour.

Today these races still occur and many Saudis, mainly males, attend these events throughout the country. Sometimes as many as 2,000 animals are entered in these races, which often stretch many miles through the harsh desert. The most popular camel race occurs during the country's only nationally recognized annual festival, the Jenadriyah Heritage and Culture

Festival, held near Riyadh. The two-week festival, which reflects Saudi Arabians' commitment to preserving their traditional heritage, fittingly opens with the camel race.

Saudi Arabia also hosts modern sporting contests. Teenagers enjoy sports such as volleyball, baseball, basketball, table tennis, archery, and—Saudi Arabia's most popular sport—futbol (soccer). To support these sports, the Saudi government has constructed stadiums and sports complexes in practically every city and small town. In many of the country's large cities, the nation has erected "Sports Cities"—gigantic complexes with Olympic-size swimming pools, indoor and outdoor stadiums with seating for

Public parks provide the perfect spot to play—and watch—a casual futbol game.

thousands of people, playgrounds, multi-purpose courts, and sports clinics. These facilities are open to the public and are popular among male teens who might gather for a game of basketball or soccer. On weekends, thousands of Saudi men, young and old, converge on these facilities to cheer on their favorite Saudi professional soccer teams.

Coffee Shops & Shopping Malls

In addition to sports complexes, Saudi teens have two other popular hangouts: the coffee shop and the mall. Like all public places in Saudi Arabia, these two well-liked meeting spots tend to be segregated according to gender.

On any given day in a Saudi city, teenage boys pack the local coffee-houses. There are two kinds of coffee-houses teens frequent: Western-style places like Starbucks, which also have a family section for women; and more traditional all-male coffeehouses. These coffeehouses are often stuffed with men and teenage boys eating, chatting, and watching TV. An especially popular time to find teens at the coffeehouses is when a big sports game is being televised. Whether it's for the American Super Bowl or soccer's World Cup, young men gather at the shops to cheer as loud as they want for their favorite teams.

Teenage girls may not want to join in the coffeehouse fun, but they certainly can and do gather for a pastime popular among girls throughout the

More than 40 American-based Starbucks have appeared throughout the kingdom.

world: shopping! The kingdom is home to large shopping malls full of high-fashion clothing stores, food courts, and discount stores. The modern complexes are similar to malls in the West, only, again, the sexes are separated. Because unrelated people of the opposite sex are not supposed to

mingle, men and women only shop with other members of the same sex or with their families.

Teen girls are often the malls' most prevalent patrons. Groups of young women, sometimes accompanied by a chaperone, trot through the malls' long hallways, gig- gling, gossiping, and scavenging for the best buys. Although women must cover their clothes with an abaya when leaving the home, many wear Western-style clothes at home, and some teenage girls spend a great deal of time and money buying the most popular fashions.

Shopping at the Souq

souq
sook

Saudi Arabia's traditional shopping markets are called *souqs*. Here a person receives a strong sense of the country's history. Prices are not set, so the souqs always fill with the sounds of people bargaining for purchases. Shoppers can buy fresh Arabian produce, traditional Bedouin handicrafts, musical instruments, tents, incense, and even gold. The souqs remain a place of great activity, with children scurrying about, men and women haggling over prices, and vendors stockpiling goods. Despite the construction of modern shopping malls, souqs continue to be popular.

Shopping malls like the al-Faysalia mall in Riyadh can be quite crowded before important holidays such as Eid al-Fitr.

One former Saudi student said that today, despite strict rules concerning gender segregation, malls have become a popular place for teens to go "numbering":

"This is where boys and girls exchange cell phone numbers in malls and streets and get to call each other to flirt and sometimes fall in love!"

From a distance, these teens throw wadded-up pieces of paper with their numbers on them to members of the opposite sex. The scene somewhat resembles spitball fights.

Hanging Out at Home

Because of the many restrictions on Saudi social lives, Saudi teens often spend their free time hanging out at home, enjoying the company of family and close friends. And why wouldn't they, considering a large number of Saudi homes have big-screen TVs, satellite dishes, computers, and video games?

Saudi television offers local stations with programming that remains consistent with conservative cultural and religious norms. But an estimated 80 percent of Saudi city dwellers own satellite dishes. The dishes allow Saudi teens to watch movies and television programs from all over the world. American television is quite popular among Saudi teens. In fact, according to the *Wall Street Journal*, America's talk show queen Oprah Winfrey has found

Playing pool is a popular pastime with some Saudi teens. In private homes, boys and girls can challenge each other to a game.

a devoted young female audience in Saudi Arabia. And while Hollywood movies cannot be shown on the big cinema screen, they are easily attainable for Saudi teenagers with the click of the satellite remote or a quick trip to the video store.

Most Saudi teens are familiar with modern technology. Cell phones, iPods, and other MP3 players have made their way into the everyday lives of most teens. Many also spend a great deal of time on the Internet looking up information and chatting with friends from different parts of the world. As of 2005, Saudi Arabia had more than 2.5 million Internet users.

However, the Internet is highly censored by the Saudi government, which has installed

filtering systems to block Saudi Internet subscribers from viewing any "inappropriate" content. The government blocks sexually explicit content, Web pages having to do with religions other than Islam, and anti-Saudi sites.

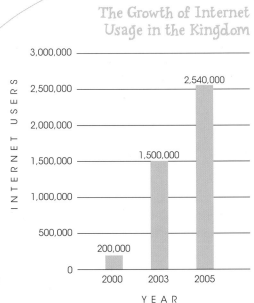

The Growth of Internet Usage in the Kingdom

Source: Internet World Stats

Saudi Censorship

Government censorship in the country does not end with the Internet. Government officials go to great lengths to censor and limit all written material and media communications in the country. The government feels this censorship protects citizens from items and ideas that are considered inappropriate or spiritually harmful under Islamic law.

Newspapers, magazines, and books are all subject to Saudi censorship. Eleven major newspapers exist in the country. Each is largely influenced by government officials who make sure nothing is printed that might damage Saudi patriotism or be considered indecent. Foreign magazines and other publications are available at Saudi newsstands, but they often have gaping holes where government employees cut out anything they considered inappropriate. These censors are especially careful to remove pictures of underdressed women because it goes against Saudi culture to see the uncovered flesh of an unrelated female.

Radio is the most difficult medium for the government to regulate and censor. When teens flip on the radio, they may hear reports that normally would not make it into the newspapers. However, like teens worldwide, most Saudi teens turn on the radio to hear music. Traditionally most music has been considered sinful. However, because of satellite television, modern music has become popular among Saudi teens. Popular local musicians include Saudi Arabia's first pop star, Abdul-Majeed Abdullah, and star Mohamed Abdu, who is called the artist of the Arabs.

Mohamed Abdu

Looking Ahead

SAUDI TEENS WILL CONTINUE TO FEEL A GREAT PULL BETWEEN THE PAST AND PRESENT as their society develops. Teens today are living in a country of rapid change and great contrasts. At almost every turn, the clash between ancient and modern ideals is apparent. And today's Saudi teens must decide how to, or if they should, continue to reconcile this balance.

Social ideals in the kingdom are changing. Teens already have witnessed major developments. They have seen more and more women enter higher education and the workforce. And though they live in a country steeped in conservatism, they have been bombarded with state-of-the-art technology and Western influences like Oprah and MTV.

Saudi teens are experiencing a very exciting time in their country's history—a time when opportunities are mounting. Today's teens will shape the future of Saudi Arabia. The responsibility of keeping their nation moving forward, while still maintaining strong traditional and religious norms, lies with them.

Official name: Kingdom of Saudi Arabia

Capital: Riyadh

People

Population: 27,019,731 (Figure includes 5,576,076 foreign residents.)

Population by age group:
0-14 years: 38.2%
15-64 years: 59.4%
65 and up: 2.4%

Life expectancy at birth: 75.67 years

Official language: Arabic

Religion: Islam (The government identifies 100% of the population as Muslim.)

Legal ages:
Alcohol consumption: Illegal for all ages
Driving license: 18 (males only)
Driving permit: 17 (males only)
Employment: 13
Marriage: no minimum
Military service: After high school graduation (males only)
Voting: 21 (males only)

Government

Type of government: Monarchy

Chief of state: King

Head of government: King

Lawmaking body: Majlis al-Shura (Consultative Council), appointed by the monarch

Administrative divisions: 13 provinces

Independence: September 23, 1932 (unification of the kingdom)

National symbols: In the national emblem, swords symbolize courage, strength, and determination, and the date palm symbolizes life and prosperity.

Geography

Total area: 784,233 square miles (1,960,582 square kilometers)

Climate: Desert climate with extreme temperature changes

Highest point: Jabal Sawda', 10,339 feet (3,133 meters)

Lowest point: Persian Gulf, sea level

Major rivers: No permanent rivers or streams

Major landforms: Rub' Al Khali Desert, An-Nafud Desert, Hejaz and Azir mountain ranges

Economy

Currency: Saudi riyal

Major natural resources: Petroleum, natural gas, gold, copper, and iron ore

Major agricultural products: Wheat, barley, tomatoes, melons, dates, chickens, eggs, milk

Major exports: Petroleum and petroleum products account for 90 percent of the kingdom's exports

Major imports: Machinery and equipment, food, chemicals, motor vehicles, textiles

Historical Timeline

The prophet Muhammad is born in Mecca

 Inca civilization flourishes in South America

The sons of Muhammad al Saud attack and capture the holy cities of Mecca and Medina; for the next 60 years, they continue to conquer land and extend their authority in Arabia

Abdul Aziz ibn Saud marches warriors into his family's former regions; he continues to conquer land throughout Arabia for the next 20 years

 World War I

| 360 | 570 | c. 1000 | 1500s | 1802–1804 | 1871–1887 | 1902 | 1914–1918 |

  Huns invade Europe

Ottoman Turks rule much of what is today Saudi Arabia

The Al Sauds begin to lose control of their regions to the Ottomans and to the Al Rashids, a rival family

 Historical World Event

Oil is discovered

King Faisal is assassinated
by his nephew Prince
Faisal ibn Musaid;
Faisal's half-brother
Khalid becomes
king; when Khalid
dies in 1982, his
half-brother Fahd
becomes king

King Abdul Aziz dies; his
eldest son, Saud, takes
over the throne

King Saud is
removed from
power; his half-
brother Faisal
becomes king

 World War II

| 1932 | 1938 | 1939–1945 | 1950–1953 | 1953 | 1960 | 1963 | 1964 | 1975 |

The Korean War

The first girls'
school opens in
the kingdom

The Kingdom of Saudi Arabia
is founded, and Abdul Aziz
becomes king

Saudi Arabia is one of
the founding members
of the Organization of
Petroleum Exporting
Countries (OPEC)

Historical Timeline

 Huge tsunami strikes nations bordering the Indian Ocean, killing more than 150,000 people and leaving millions homeless

More than 360 Hajj pilgrims are crushed to death during a stone throwing ritual

Osama bin Ladin, a Saudi native and head of the al-Qaeda militant group that later instigated the 2001 terrorist attacks against the United States, is stripped of his Saudi citizenship

1990	1991	1994	2001	2004	2005	2006

Saudi Arabia holds its first open elections; in August, King Fahd dies; his brother Abdullah takes over as king

Iraq attacks Kuwait; Saudi Arabia becomes part of the coalition of countries fighting to protect Kuwait during the Persian Gulf War

Terrorists attack the United States; Saudi Arabia discovers that 15 of the 19 airline hijackers were Saudi citizens

Soviet Union collapses

Glossary

amenities | items that add pleasantness or comfort

curriculum | the courses of study offered at an educational institution

gross domestic product | the total value of all goods and services produced in a country during a specific period

lunar | measurement based on the revolution of the moon

mosque | the Muslim place of worship

nationals | citizens of a particular country

nomad | a herder who travels from place to place looking for favorable pastureland, never settling in one place for long

pilgrimage | a journey to a holy place

Qur'an | the holy book of Islam, which consists mainly of the revelations Muhammad received from God during the seventh century

Sabbath | the day of the week when religious services are held

segregation | the practice of separating different groups of people; for example, separating males from females

vocational school | a school that prepares students to enter a particular field of employment, usually a field that requires skilled workers such as mechanics, plumbers, or carpenters

Additional Resources

IN THE LIBRARY

Barnes, Trevor. *Islam: Worship, Festivals, and Ceremonies from Around the World*. New York: Kingfisher, 2005.

Broberg, Catherine. *Saudi Arabia in Pictures*. Minneapolis: Lerner Publications, 2003.

Harper, Robert A. *Saudi Arabia*. Philadelphia: Chelsea House, 2003.

Keating, Susan Katz. *Saudi Arabia*. Philadelphia: Mason Crest Publishers., 2004.

Losleben, Elizabeth. *The Bedouin of the Middle East*. Minneapolis: Lerner Publications, 2003.

Reed, Jennifer. *The Saudi Royal Family*. New York: Chelsea House, 2006.

Schaffer, David. *Saudi Arabia in the News: Past, Present, and Future*. Berkeley Heights, N.J.: MyReportLinks.com Books, 2006.

ON THE WEB

For more information on this topic, use FactHound.

1. Go to www.facthound.com
2. Type in this book ID: 0756520665
3. Click on the Fetch It button.

Look for more Global Connections books.

Teens in Australia
Teens in Brazil
Teens in China
Teens in France
Teens in India
Teens in Israel
Teens in Japan

Teens in Kenya
Teens in Mexico
Teens in Russia
Teens in Spain
Teens in Venezuela
Teens in Vietnam

Source Notes

Page 19, column 2, line 10: Kingdom of Saudi Arabia. Ministry of Culture and Information. The Saudi Arabia Information Resource. "King Fahd: Some Quotations." 12 July 2006. www.saudinf.com/main/b467.htm

Page 26, column 2, line 4: Manal Quota, "How Saudis Grow Up Without Learning Household Chores." Arab News. 8 Aug. 2005. 27 June 2006. www.arabnews.com/?page=1&section=0&article=68086

Page 37. column 1, line 12: Aisha Sultan. "Islamic Foundation Turns to Youth." STLtoday.com. 8 July 2006. 13 July 2006. www.stltoday.com/stltoday/news/stories.nsf/religion/story/1B1C4C33F5FDCF862571A5000674C0?OpenDocument

Page 55, column 2, line 4: David E. Long. *Cultures and Customs of Saudi Arabia*. Westport, Conn.: Greenwood Press, 2005, p. 69.

Page 63, line 35: "Transcript: Saudi King Abdullah Talks to Barbara Walters: New Ruler Addresses Oil Prices, Al Qaeda, and Women's Rights." ABC News. 14 Oct. 2005. 7 July 2006. http://abcnews.go.com/2020/International/story?id=1214706&page=1

Page 79, column 1, line 6: Anonymous former Saudi student. E-mail interview. 13 Feb. 2006.

Pages 84–85, At a Glance: United States. Central Intelligence Agency. *The World Factbook—Saudi Arabia*. 17 Oct. 2006. 27 Oct. 2006. www.cia.gov/cia/publications/factbook/geos/sa.html

Select Bibliography

Ahmad, Mahmoud. "Taking Teenagers Off the Streets." *Arab News* 4 Jan. 2005. 18 Jan. 2006. www.arabnews.com/?page=1&section=0&article=57049&d=4&m=1&y=2005

Bosbait, Muhammed, and Rodney Wilson. "Education, School to Work Transitions and Unemployment in Saudi Arabia." *Middle Eastern Studies* 41.4. July 2005. pp. 533-545.

Bradley, John R. *Saudi Arabia Exposed: Inside a Kingdom in Crisis*. New York: Palgrave McMillan, 2005.

"Education in the Arab States: Five Million Girls Still Denied Access to School." *United Nations Educational Scientific and Cultural Organization*. 14 May 2003. 10 Jan. 2006. http://domino.un.org/UNISPAL.NSF/0/16e7c1ce7a805ffe85256d2800528760?OpenDocument

Human Rights Watch World Report 2002: Saudi Arabia. 27 June 2006. http://hrw.org/wr2k2/mena7.html

Kingdom of Saudi Arabia. Ministry of Culture and Information. The Saudi Arabia Information Resource. "King Fahd: Some Quotations." 12 July 2006. www.saudinf.com/main/b467.htm

Long, David E. *Cultures and Customs of Saudi Arabia*. Westport, Conn.: Greenwood Press, 2005.

Mackey, Sandra. *The Saudis: Inside a Desert Kingdom*. New York: Norton, 2002.

Quota, Manal. "How Saudis Grow Up Without Learning Household Chores." *Arab News* 8 Aug. 2005. 27 June 2006. www.arabnews.com/?page=1&section=0&article=68086

"Saudi Arabia: Educational Overview." *World Education Profiles*. 6 May 2004. 10 Jan. 2006. www.wes.org/ca/wedb/saudiarabia/saedov.htm

"Saudi Arabia Internet Usage and Marketing Report." Internet World Stats. 30 Oct. 2006. www.internetworldstats.com/me/sa.htm

"Saudi Arabia: Largest Cities and Towns and Statistics of Their Population." World Gazetteer. 2006. 30 Oct. 2006. www.world-gazetteer.com/wg.php?x=&men=gcis&lng=en&dat=32&geo=-185&srt=npan&col=aohdq&pt=c&va=&srt=pnan

"Saudi Arabia: Youth Literacy Rate." UN Common Database. Globalis–Saudi Arabia. 30 Oct. 2006. http://globalis.gvu.unu.edu/indicator_detail.cfm?country=SA&indicatorid=18

The Saudi Information Resource. 28 June 2005. www.saudinf.com

al Shemary, Abdulaziz. "$75 Billion to Develop Saudi Educational Sector." *Asharq Alawsat.* 18 Oct. 2005. 8 Feb. 2006. www.asharqalawsat.com/english/print.asp?artid=id2235

Sultan, Aisha. "Islamic Foundation Turns to Youth." *STLtoday.com* 8 July 2006. 13 July 2006. www.stltoday.com/stltoday/news/stories.nsf/religion/story/81B14C33F5FDCF862571A5000674C0?OpenDocument

"Transcript: Saudi King Abdullah Talks to Barbara Walters: New Ruler Addresses Oil Prices, Al Qaeda, and Women's Rights." *ABC News.* 14 Oct. 2005. 7 July 2006. http://abcnews.go.com/2020/International/story?id=1214706&page=1

United States. Central Intelligence Agency. *The World Factbook—Saudi Arabia.* 17 Oct. 2006. 27 Oct. 2006. www.cia.gov/cia/publications/factbook/geos/sa.html

United States Department of Energy. Energy Information Administration. *Saudi Arabia Country Analysis Brief.* August 2005. 15 February 2006. www.eia.doe.gov/emeu/cabs/saudi.html

United States Department of State. Bureau of Consular Affairs. *Saudi Arabia.* December 2005. 16 Dec. 2005. http://travel.state.gov/travel/cis_pa_tw/cis/cis_1012.html

Wilson, Peter W., and Douglas F. Graham. *Saudi Arabia: The Coming Storm.* New York: M.E. Sharpe, 1994.

Index

About the Author
Nicki Yackley-Franken

Nicki Yackley-Franken recently graduated with a master of arts degree in English from Minnesota State University, Mankato. In addition to being an author, she has worked as a journalist and a composition instructor. Raised in Sioux Center, Iowa, Nicki currently lives in Watertown, South Dakota.

About the Content Adviser
Christopher Rose, M.A.

Our content adviser for *Teens in Saudi Arabia,* Christopher Rose, speaks Arabic—the native language of Saudi Arabia. His academic interests are Islamic history and multicultural education. As the Outreach Coordinator for the Center of Middle Eastern Studies at the University of Texas at Austin, he frequently speaks to community and school groups with the goal of enhancing knowledge and understanding of the Middle East. Rose's involvement with this book was perfectly timed to coincide with a visit to Saudi Arabia.